Viv the hen was not in the pen.

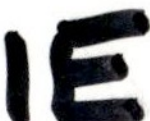

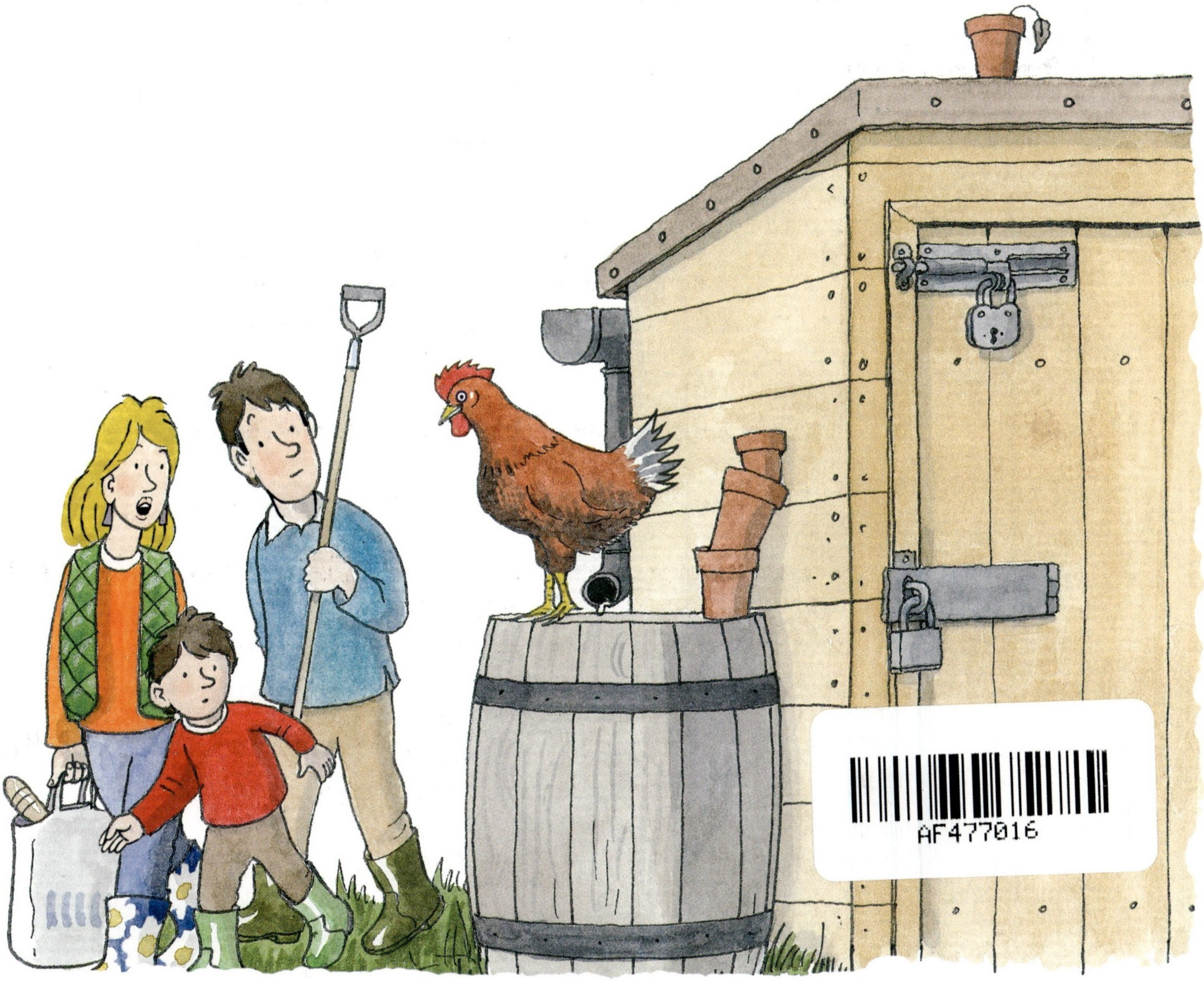

1

Dad had a net.

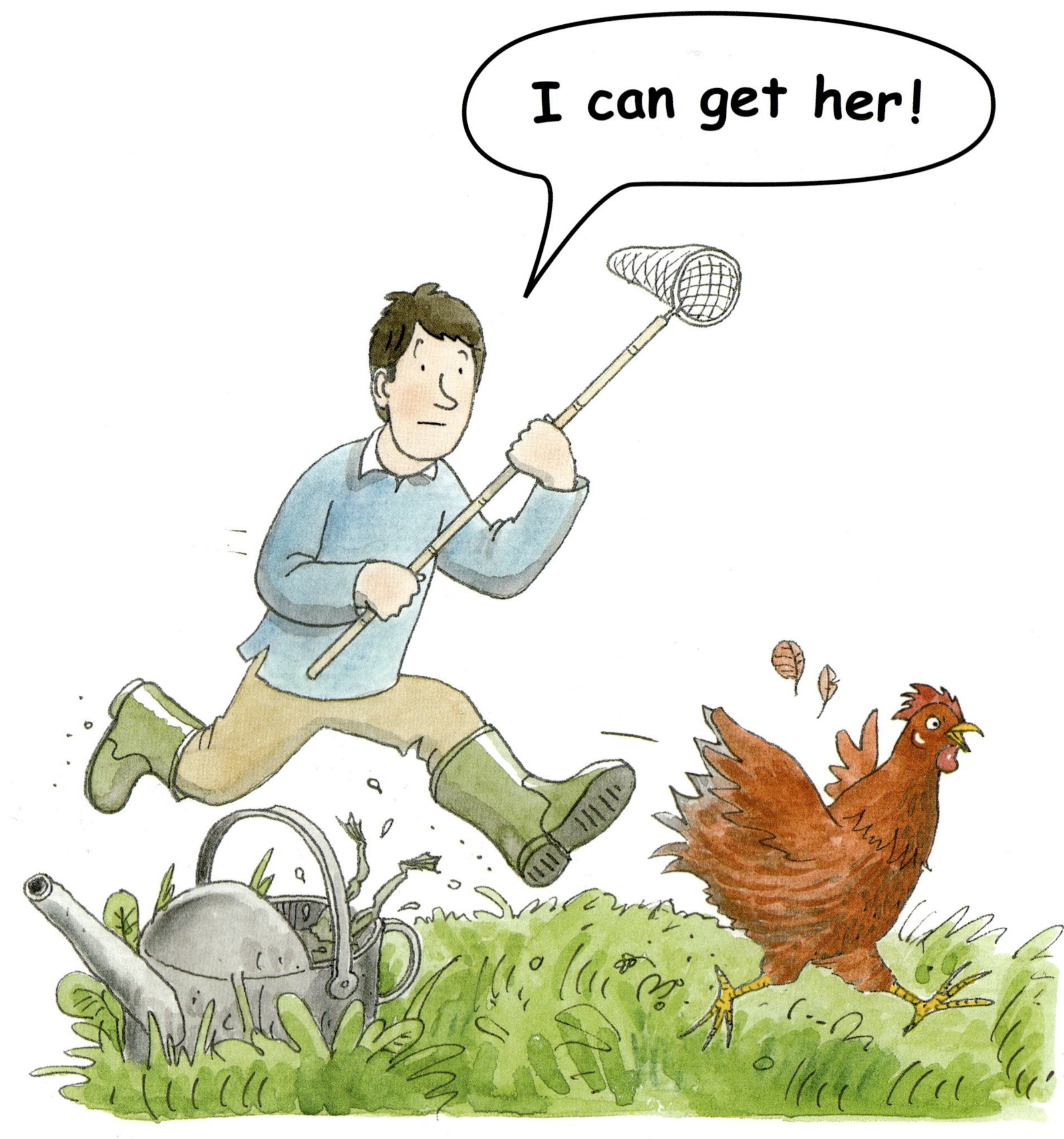

2

Mum had a bag.

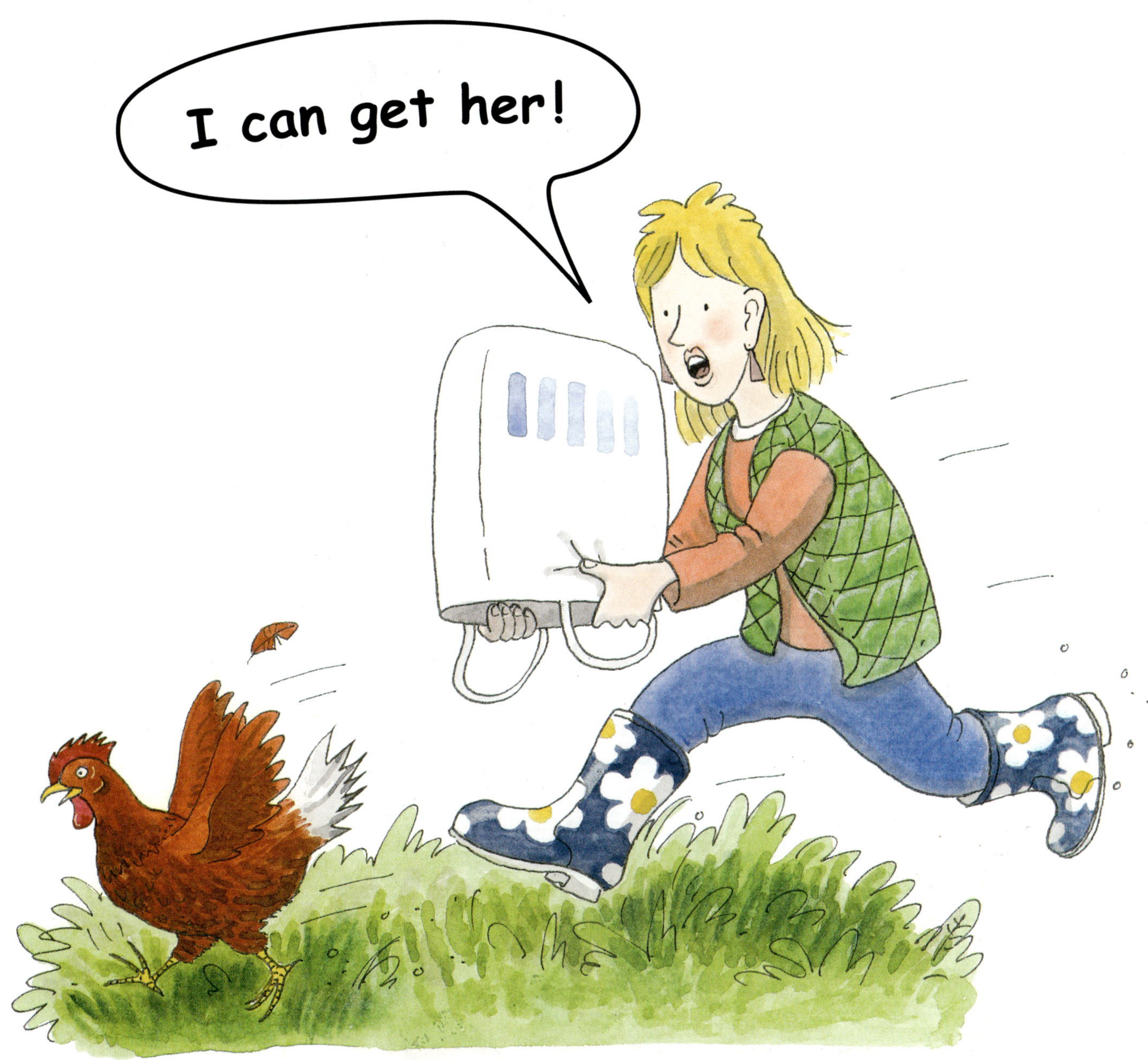

Viv ran.
Mum ran and Dad ran.

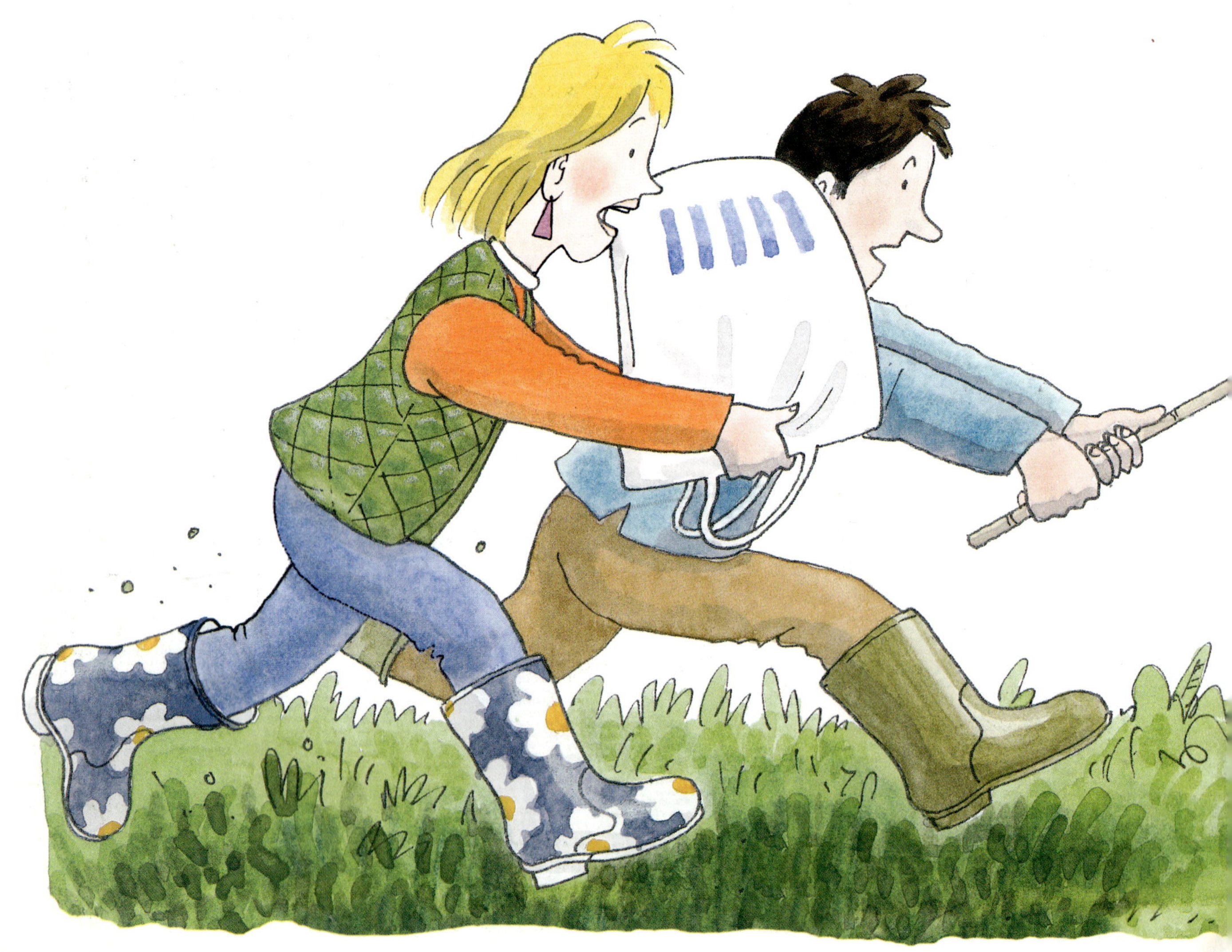

"Let me get her," said Chip.

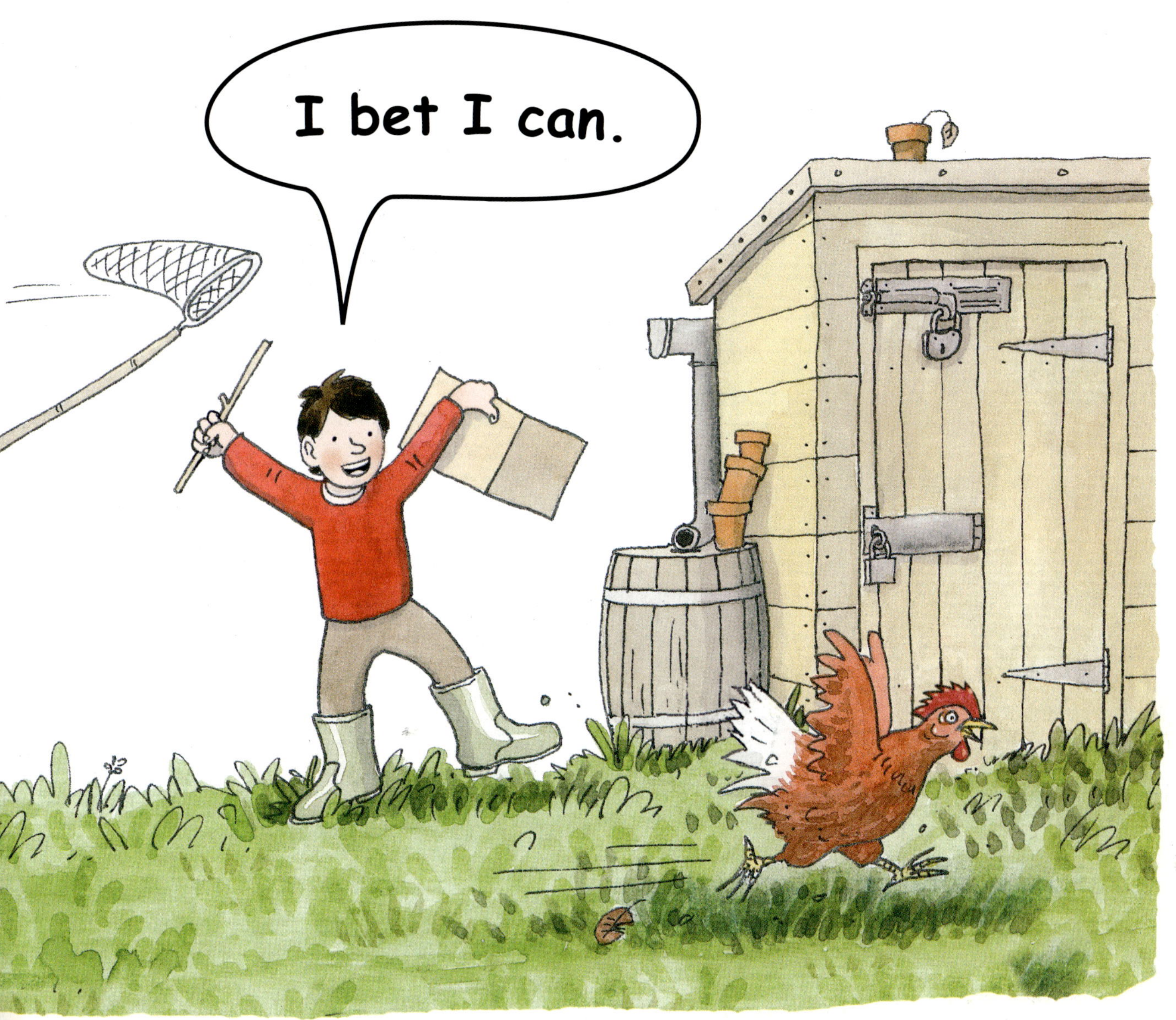

Chip got a big box.

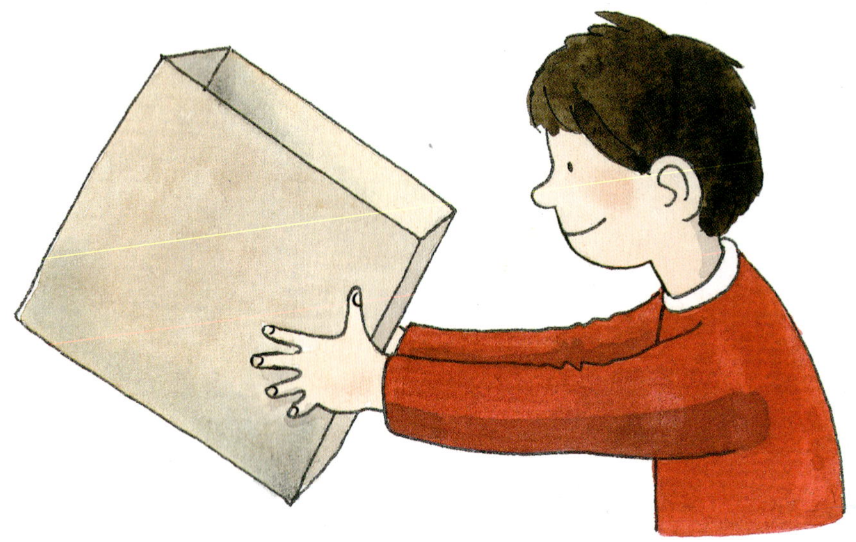

He set the box up.

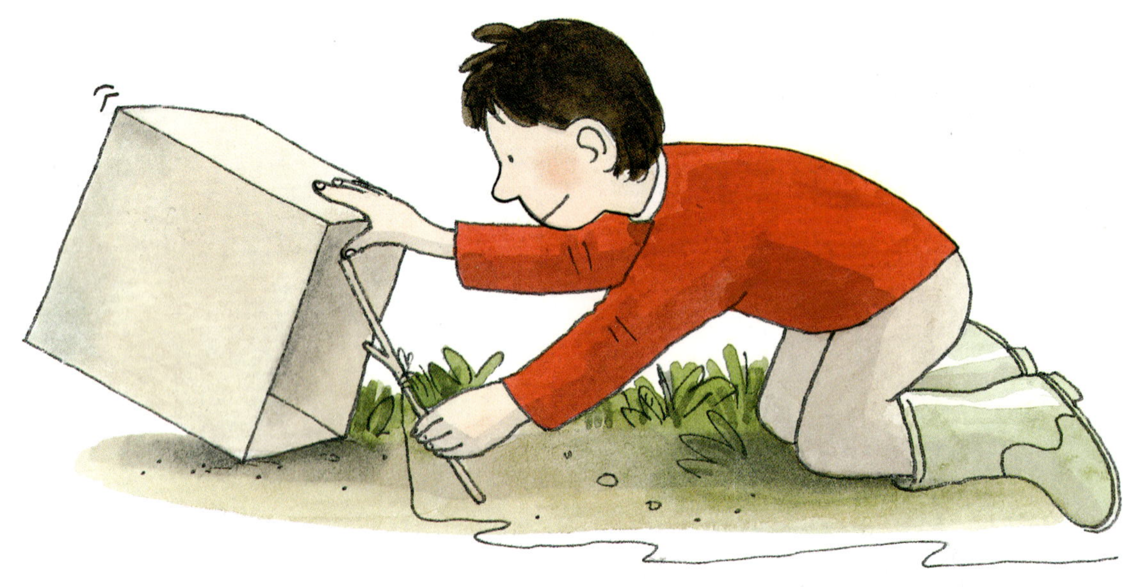

He put in a pot.

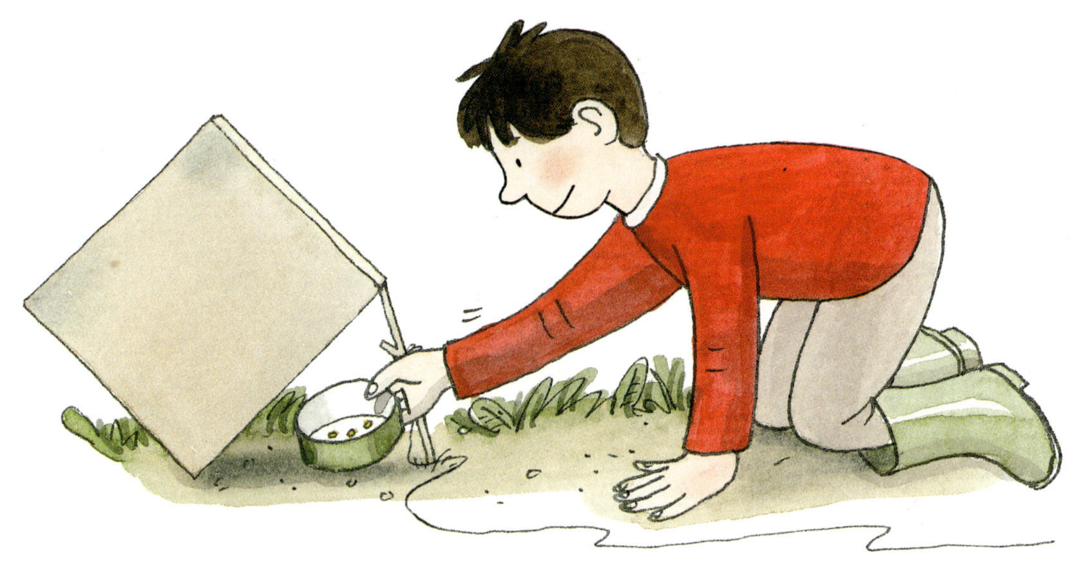

Chip got Viv in the box.

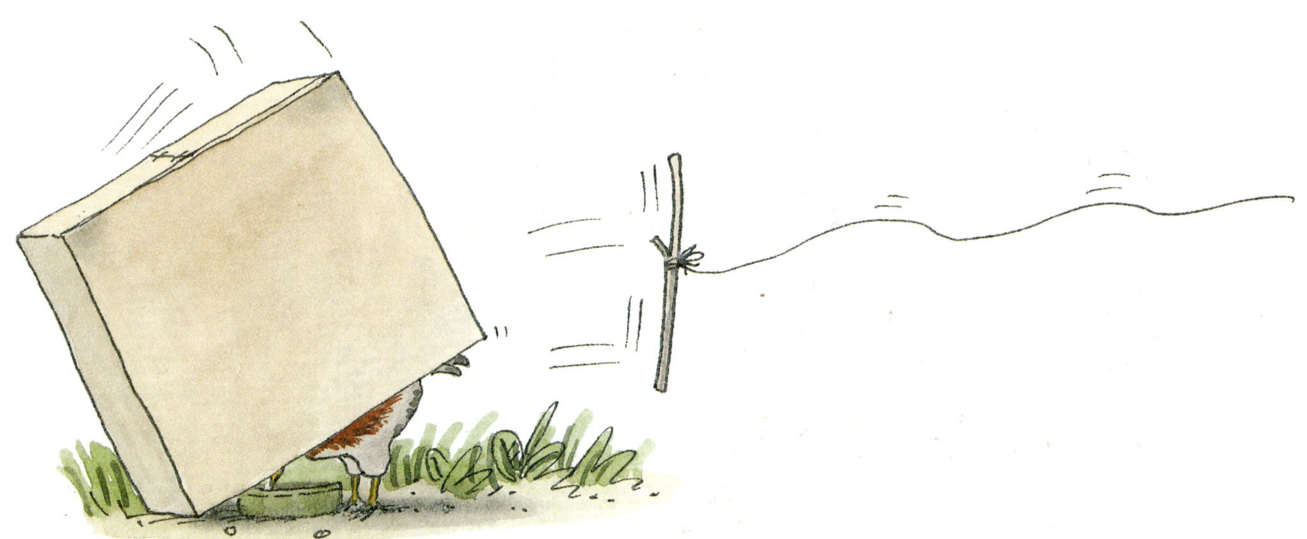

Dad put Viv in the pen.

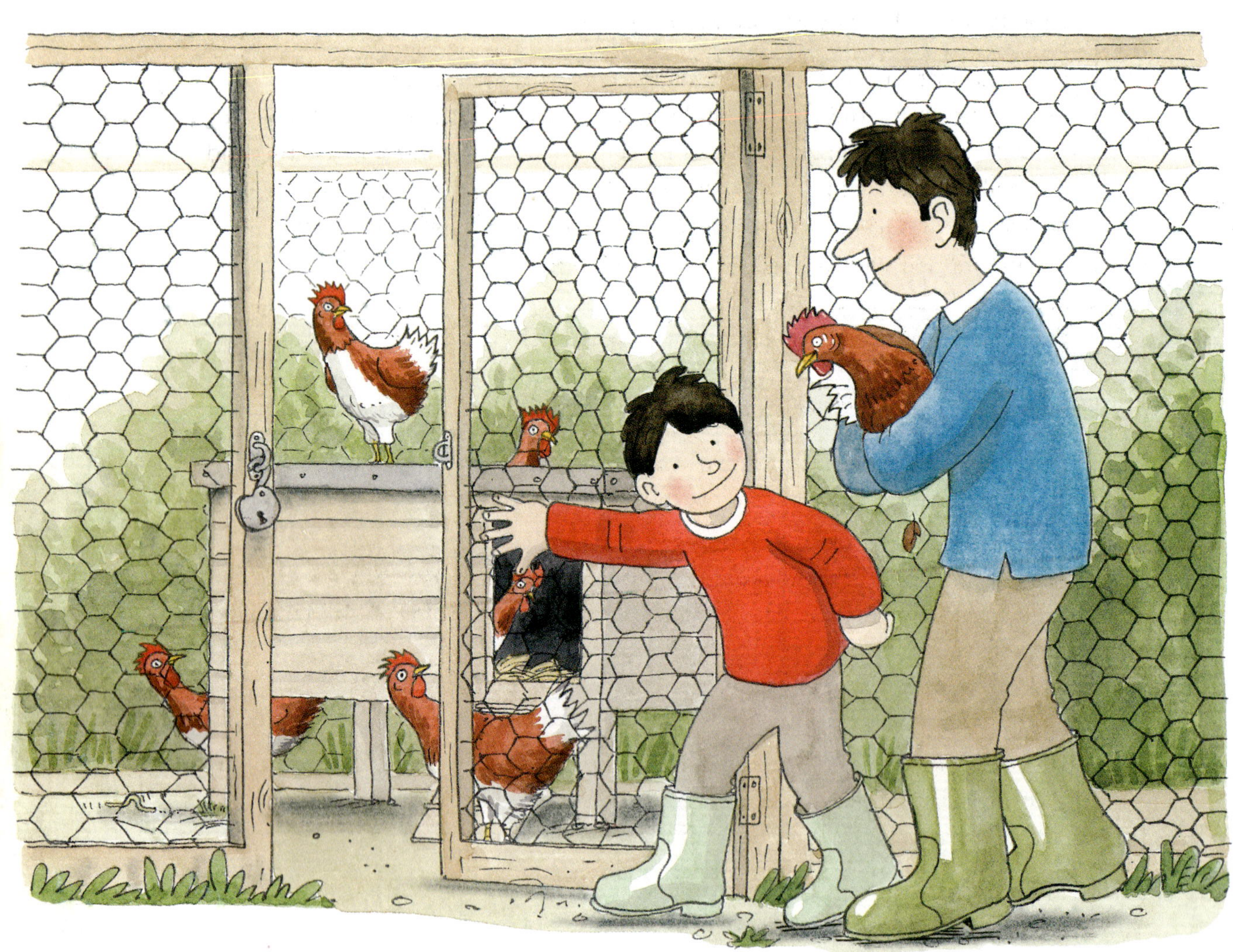